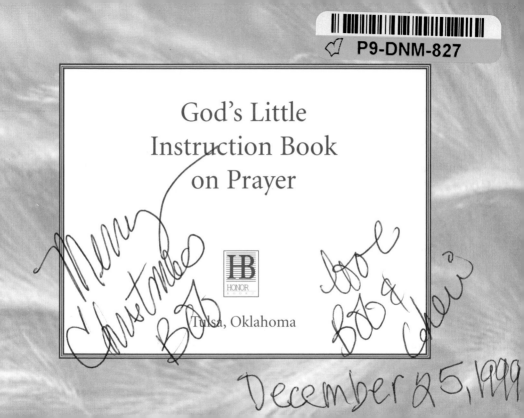

God's Little
Instruction Book
on Prayer

HB
HONOR
BOOKS

Tulsa, Oklahoma

Merry Christmas
Bob

Love
Bob & Cheri

December 25, 1999

8th Printing

God's Little Instruction Book on Prayer
ISBN 1-56292-002-2
Copyright © 1996 by Honor Books, Inc.
P. O. Box 55388
Tulsa, Oklahoma 74155

Manuscript prepared by W. B. Freeman Concepts, Inc., Tulsa, Oklahoma.

Introduction

The human heart instinctively longs for fellowship with God. We *desire* to communicate with our Creator. In simplest terms, this communication is called prayer.

Through the centuries men and women have expressed their beliefs about prayer. From the context of their own lives, they have valued prayer as their link to heaven, a holy practice which produces tremendous benefits in all areas of life.

Most important, prayer establishes and deepens your personal relationship with God. No other relationship is more valuable — not only in your daily life, but for all eternity.

May *God's Little Instruction Book on Prayer* encourage you as you develop your relationship with your Heavenly Father.

Since therefore, brethren, we have confidence to enter the holy place by the blood of Jesus,...let us draw near with a sincere heart in full assurance of faith.
Hebrews 10:19,22
NASB

Beware of placing the emphasis on what prayer costs us; it cost God everything to make it possible for us to pray.

4

Prayer requires that we stand in God's presence ...proclaiming to ourselves and to others that without God we can do nothing.

He who abides in Me, and I in him, bears much fruit; for without Me you can do nothing.
John 15:5 NKJV

5

Then Jonah prayed unto the Lord his God out of the fish's belly.
Jonah 2:1

Prayer is profitable wherever it is invested.

I know not by what methods rare, But this I know: God answers prayer.

Then you shall call, and the Lord will answer; you shall cry for help, and he will say, Here I am.
Isaiah 58:9 NRSV

Therefore let everyone who is godly pray to you while you may be found; surely when the mighty waters rise, they will not reach him.
Psalm 32:6 NIV

The best advice my mother ever gave me — don't forget to say your prayers.

Prayer is a direct link to peace of mind and perspective. It reminds us of who we are.

Trust in the Lord with all your heart, And lean not on your own understanding; In all your ways acknowledge him, And he shall direct your paths.
Proverbs 3:5-6
NKJV

And pray in the Spirit on all occasions with all kinds of prayers and requests.
Ephesians 6:18
NIV

True prayer is a way of life, not just in case of emergency.

We should never pray without reading the Bible, and we should never read the Bible without praying.

For the reverence and fear of God are basic to all wisdom. Knowing God results in every other kind of understanding.
Proverbs 9:10 TLB

Be merciful unto me, O Lord; for I cry unto thee daily.
Psalm 86:3

I do not always bend the knee to pray; I often pray in crowded city street in some hard crisis of a busy day — prayer is my sure and comforting retreat.

Here at my office desk I ask His aid, no matter where I am I crave His care; in moments when my soul is sore afraid it comforts most to know He's everywhere.

Seek the Lord and his strength, seek his face continually.
1 Chronicles 16:11

*Commit your way
to the Lord,
Trust also in
Him, and He
shall bring it
to pass.*
Psalm 37:5 NKJV

Our business in prayer is not to prescribe but to subscribe to the wisdom and will of God; to refer our case to Him, and then leave it with Him.

The prayer that begins with trustfulness, and passes on into waiting, will always end in thankfulness, triumph, and praise.

Elijah was a man with a nature like ours, and he prayed earnestly that it might not rain; and it did not rain.
James 5:17 NASB

We receive from Him whatever we ask, because we [watchfully] obey His orders...and [habitually] practice what is pleasing to Him.
1 John 3:22 AMP

When we serve the Lord with our whole heart, we have confidence and joy in prayer.

To pray does not only mean to seek help; it also means to seek Him.

Your face, Lord, do I seek.
Psalm 27:8 NRSV

Let us not grow weary while doing good, for in due season we shall reap if we do not lose heart.
Galatians 6:9
NKJV

Time spent in prayer is never wasted.

By far the most important thing about praying is to keep at it.

Then Jesus told them a parable about their need to pray always and not to lose heart.
Luke 18:1 NRSV

The Lord is righteous in all his ways...He fulfills the desires of those who fear him; he hears their cry and saves them.
Psalm 145:17,19
NIV

∽

The most praying souls are the most assured souls.

Prayer crowns God with the honor and glory due to His name, and God crowns prayer with assurance and comfort.

I will exalt you, my God the King ...and extol your name for ever and ever. Great is the Lord and most worthy of praise; his greatness no one can fathom.
Psalm 145:1-3
NIV

God looks not at the oratory of your prayers, how elegant they may be; nor at the geometry of your prayers, how long they may be; nor at the arithmetic of your prayers, how many they may be; nor at logic of your prayers, how methodical they may be; but the sincerity of them.

In Christ we speak as persons of sincerity.
2 Corinthians 2:17 NRSV

The fewer words the better prayer.

And when you pray, do not use vain repetitions as the heathen do. For they think that they will be heard for their many words. Therefore do not be like them.
Matthew 6:7-8
NKJV

We know that all things work together for good for those who love God, who are called according to his purpose.
Romans 8:28
NRSV

Prayer is the chief agency and activity whereby men align themselves with God's purpose.

Prayer is not only "the practice of the presence of God," it is the realization of His presence.

Thou wilt make known to me the path of life; in Thy presence is fulness of joy.
Psalm 16:11 NASB

When they saw the courage of Peter and John and realized that they were unschooled, ordinary men, they were astonished and they took note that these men had been with Jesus.
Acts 4:13 NIV

∾

No Christian is greater than his prayer life.

The first purpose of prayer is to know God.

*I lift up my eyes to the hills —
where does my help come from?
My help comes from the Lord, the Maker of heaven and earth.
Psalm 121:1-2
NIV*

Devote yourselves to prayer, keeping alert in it with an attitude of thanksgiving.
Colossians 4:2
NASB

∼

As artists give themselves to their models, and poets to their classical pursuits, so must we addict ourselves to prayer.

He who fails to pray does not cheat God. He cheats himself.

Blessed is the man who reveres God, but the man who doesn't care is headed for serious trouble.
Proverbs 28:14
TLB

29

I would know the words which he would answer me, and understand what he would say unto me.
Job 23:5

If you would have God hear you when you pray, you must hear Him when He speaks.

The value of persistent prayer is not that He will hear us...but that we will finally hear Him.

Incline your ear, and come to Me. Hear, and your soul shall live. Isaiah 55:3 NKJV

*Draw near to
God and He will
draw near
to you.*
James 4:8 NASB

Prayer is a rising up and a drawing near to God in mind, and in heart, and in spirit.

A s breath is to the body, prayer is to the soul.

I called upon thy name, O Lord... hide not thine ear at my breathing.
Lamentations 3:55-56

Love your enemies, bless them that curse you, do good to them that hate you, and pray for them which despitefully use you, and persecute you.
Matthew 5:44

Prayer can change what arguments can't settle.

If Christians spent as much time praying as they do grumbling, they would soon have nothing to grumble about.

Do all things without grumbling or disputing; that you may prove yourselves to be blameless and innocent, children of God.
Philippians 2:14,15 NASB

Hear my prayer,
O Lord, and
let my cry
come to You.
Psalm 102:1 NKJV

Prayer is the wing wherewith the soul flies to heaven.

I f trouble drives you to prayer, prayer will drive the trouble away.

The Lord is a refuge for the oppressed, a stronghold in times of trouble.
Psalm 9:9 NIV

Keep watching and praying, that you may not enter into temptation; the spirit is willing, but the flesh is weak.
Matthew 26:41
NASB

Leave not off praying to God: for either praying will make thee leave off sinning; or continuing in sin will make thee desist from praying.

Do not our prayers for help mean: Help me to be better than I know myself to be.

If we confess our sins, He is faithful and just to forgive us our sins and to cleanse us from all unrighteousness.
1 John 1:9 NKJV

39

If my people who are called by my name humble themselves, pray, seek my face, and turn from their wicked ways, then I will hear from heaven, and will forgive their sin and heal their land.
2 Chronicles 7:14
NRSV

Humility is the principal aid to prayer.

40

Between the humble and contrite heart and the majesty of heaven there are no barriers; the only password is prayer.

But this is the one to whom I will look, to the humble and contrite in spirit, who trembles at my word.
Isaiah 66:2 NRSV

One of his disciples said to him, "Lord, teach us to pray."
Luke 11:1 NRSV

There are few men who dare to publish to the world the prayers they make to Almighty God.

Just when I need Him, He is my all, answering when upon Him I call; tenderly watching lest I should fall.

And God is able to make all grace abound toward you; that ye, always having all sufficiency in all things, may abound to every good work.
2 Corinthians 9:8

Every good and holy desire, though it lack the form, hath in itself the substance and force of a prayer with God, who regardeth the very moanings, groans, and sighings of the heart.

...for out of the abundance of the heart the mouth speaketh.
Matthew 12:34

44

Prayer always gets through to God no matter where a person might be.

From the depths...I called for help, and you listened to my cry.
Jonah 2:2 NIV

If our consciences are clear, we can come to the Lord with perfect assurance and trust.
1 John 3:21 TLB

If our heart is far from God, the words of prayer are in vain.

Prayer unites the soul to God.

O My Father, if it is possible, let this cup pass from Me; nevertheless, not as I will, but as You will.
Matthew 26:39
NKJV

Beloved, I wish above all things that thou mayest prosper and be in health, even as thy soul prospereth.
3 John 2

Prayer is not overcoming God's reluctance; it is laying hold of His highest willingness.

Praying without faith is like trying to cut with a blunt knife — much labour expended to little purpose.

But ask in faith, never doubting, for the one who doubts is like a wave of the sea, driven and tossed by the wind.
James 1:6 NRSV

And the Lord
turned the
captivity of Job,
when he prayed
for his friends.
Job 42:10

Prayer changes
everything: It changes
the one who prays, and it
changes the one prayed for.

Prayer does not change God, but changes him who prays.

For I am the Lord, I do not change.
Malachi 3:6 AMP

For there is not a word in my tongue, but, lo, O Lord, thou knowest it altogether.
Psalm 139:4

The deepest wishes of the heart find expression in secret prayer.

Prayer — secret, fervent, believing prayer — lies at the root of all personal godliness.

Epaphras, who is one of you, a servant of Christ, saluteth you, always labouring fervently for you in prayers, that ye may stand perfect and complete in all the will of God. Colossians 4:12

Likewise the Spirit also helps in our weaknesses. For we do not know what we should pray for as we ought....
Romans 8:26
NKJV

Prayer is a sincere, sensible, affectionate pouring out of the soul to God.

Prayer is not eloquence, but earnestness.

The Lord looks down from heaven...to see if there are any who understand, who seek God. Psalm 14:2 NKJV

And God created man in His own image, in the image of God He created him.
Genesis 1:27 NASB

Prayer is essentially man standing before his God in wonder, awe, and humility; man, made in the image of God, responding to his maker.

Prayer is the breath of the soul, the organ by which we receive Christ into our parched and withered hearts.

Blessed is the man who listens to me, watching daily at my gates, waiting at the posts of my doors. For whoever finds me finds life, and obtains favor from the Lord.
Proverbs 8:34,35
NKJV

Apply your heart to instruction, and your ears to words of knowledge.
Proverbs 23:12
NKJV

Don't bother to give God instructions; just report for duty.

God's giving is inseparably connected with our asking.

You do not have, because you do not ask.
James 4:2 NRSV

Put your hope in God, for I will yet praise him, my Savior and my God. Psalm 42:5 NIV

Prayer is a cry of hope.

I n prayer it is better to have a heart without words, than words without a heart.

And when you pray, you shall not be like the hypocrites. For they love to pray standing in the synagogues and on the corners of the streets, that they may be seen by men. Assuredly, I say to you, they have their reward.
Matthew 6:5
NKJV

...looking unto Jesus...who endured such hostility from sinners against Himself, lest you become weary and discouraged in your souls.
Hebrews 12:2,3
NKJV

To look around is to be distressed. To look within is to be depressed. To look up is to be blessed.

Praying is letting one's own heart become the place where the tears of God and the tears of God's children can merge and become tears of hope.

Blessed are those who mourn, for they shall be comforted.
Matthew 5:4
NASB

Rejoice always, pray without ceasing, in everything give thanks; for this is the will of God in Christ Jesus for you.
1 Thessalonians 5:16-18 NKJV

Human life is a constant want, and ought to be a constant prayer.

When we pray we commit ourselves to what it is we really value in the world.

But strive first for the kingdom of God and his righteousness, and all these things will be given to you as well.
Matthew 6:33
NRSV

Let, I pray thee, thy merciful kindness be for my comfort, according to thy word unto thy servant.
Psalm 119:76

Daily prayers lessen daily cares.

Make every matter of care a matter of prayer.

Casting all your care upon him; for he careth for you.
1 Peter 5:7

iving a life without
prayer is like building a
ouse without nails.

Psalm 127

68

Prayer is the channel of all blessings and the secret of power and life.

For everyone who asks, receives. Anyone who seeks, finds. If only you will knock, the door will open.
Matthew 7:8 TLB

There is a way that seems right to a man, But its end is the way of death.
Proverbs 14:12
NKJV

Nothing lies beyond the reach of prayer except that which lies beyond the will of God.

I f your prayers are sincere, then you can be sure that [your] present life is exactly what God knows is best... for you!

Lord God of Israel, there is no God in heaven or on earth like You, who keep Your covenant and mercy with Your servants who walk before You with all their hearts.
2 Chronicles 6:14
NKJV

Show the wonder of your great love, you who save by your right hand those who take refuge in you from their foes. Keep me as the apple of your eye; hide me in the shadow of your wings.
Psalm 17:7-8 NIV

Much prayer, much power. Little prayer, little power.

Strength in prayer is better than length in prayer.

I will pray with the spirit, and I will pray with the understanding also: I will sing with the spirit, and I will sing with the understanding also.
1 Corinthians 14:15

"Sun, stand still over Gibeon; and Moon, in the Valley of Aijalon." So the sun stood still, and the moon stopped. Joshua 10:12-13 NKJV

Prayer is invading the impossible.

74

Those who quietly, through prayer, used God's power, were the ones who made the world move forward.

Make progress, rise like an edifice higher and higher — praying in the Holy Spirit.
Jude 20 AMP

75

Thy kingdom come. Thy will be done, on earth as it is in heaven.
Matthew 6:10
NASB

Prayer brings [God] down to earth, and links His power with our efforts.

The sweetest lesson I have learned in God's school is to let the Lord choose for me.

For your Father knows the things you have need of before you ask Him.
Matthew 6:8
NKJV

Moses answered and said, But behold, they will not believe me... And the Lord said unto him, What is that in thine hand? And he said, A rod.
Exodus 4:1-2

Unanswered yet! Nay, do not say UNGRANTED; perhaps your part is not yet fully done.

Prayer moves the hand that moves the world.

The things which are impossible with men are possible with God.
Luke 18:27

The foolishness of is wiser than men, and the The foolishness of God is wiser than men, and the weakness of God is stronger than men.
1 Corinthians 1:25 NRSV

God's answers are wiser than our prayers.

How deeply rooted must unbelief be in our hearts when we are surprised to find our prayer answered.

Lord, I believe; help thou mine unbelief.
Mark 9:24

81

For My thoughts are not your thoughts, neither are your ways My ways, says the Lord.
Isaiah 55:8 AMP

Did not God sometimes withhold in mercy what we ask, we should be ruined at our own request.

I have lived to thank God that all my prayers have not been answered.

As the heavens are higher than the earth, so are My ways higher than your ways, and My thoughts than your thoughts.
Isaiah 55:9 NKJV

And we are sure of this, that he will listen to us whenever we ask him for anything in line with his will. And if we really know he is listening when we talk to him and make our requests, then we can be sure that he will answer us.

1 John 5:14,15
TLB

Good prayers never come creeping home. I am sure I shall receive either what I ask, or what I should ask.

Our prayer and God's mercy are like two buckets in a well; while the one ascends, the other descends.

[Jacob] dreamed that there was a ladder set up on the earth, and the top of it reached to heaven; and the angels of God were ascending and descending on it!
Genesis 28:12
AMP

Then you will call upon me and come and pray to me, and I will listen to you. You will seek me and find me when you seek me with all your heart.
Jeremiah 29:12-13
NIV

God not only gives us answers to our prayers, but with every answer gives us something of Himself.

Prayer is for the soul what nourishment is for the body.

You will keep him in perfect peace, Whose mind is stayed on You.
Isaiah 26:3 NKJV

*Wait on the Lord:
be of good
courage, and he
shall strengthen
thine hear: wait, I
say, on the Lord.
Psalm 27:14*

There are four answers to prayer: yes, no, wait, and if.

The primary purpose of prayer is not to get answers, but to deepen our friendship with God.

Abraham believed God...and he was called God's friend.
James 2:23 NIV

The effectual fervent prayer of a righteous man availeth much.
James 5:16

More things are wrought by prayer than the world dreams of.

The Christian life without prayer is like computer hardware without the software.

Call to me and I will answer you and tell you great and unsearchable things you do not know.
Jeremiah 33:3 NIV

91

...for he who comes to God must believe that He is, and that He is a rewarder of those who diligently seek Him.
Hebrews 11:6
NKJV

The answer to our prayer may be the echo of our resolve.

Prayer is a virtue that prevaileth against all temptations.

Watch and pray, lest you enter into temptation. The spirit indeed is willing, but the flesh is weak.
Mark 14:38 NKJV

The Lord has given me my petition which I asked of Him.
1 Samuel 1:27
NASB

God answers prayers because His children ask.

When God does not immediately respond to the cries of His children, it is because He wants to accomplish some gracious purpose in their lives.

...that the testing of your faith produces patience.
James 1:3 NKJV

Let us then approach the throne of grace with confidence, so that we may receive mercy and find grace to help us in our time of need. Hebrews 4:16 NIV

The greatest privilege God gives to you is the freedom to approach Him at any time.

Prayer is conversation with God.

The Lord is near to all who call upon Him, to all who call upon Him sincerely and in truth.
Psalm 145:18
AMP

But wilt thou know, O vain man, that faith without works is dead?
James 2:20

It is not well for a man to pray cream and live skim milk.

He who prays as he ought, will endeavor to live as he prays.

For those who live according to the flesh set their minds on the things of the flesh, but those who live according to the Spirit set their minds on the things of the Spirit.
Romans 8:5 NRSV

We have an advocate with the Father, Jesus Christ the righteous.
1 John 2:1

If we could hear Christ praying for us in the next room, we would have no fear. Yet distance makes no difference. He is praying for us.

They who have steeped their souls in prayer can every anguish calmly bear.

He went away again the second time, and prayed, saying, "O my Father, if this cup may not pass away from me, except I drink it, thy will be done."
Matthew 26:42

And though you have not seen Him, you love Him, and though you do not see Him now, but believe in Him, you greatly rejoice with joy inexpressible and full of glory.
1 Peter 1:8 NASB

No prayer of adoration will ever soar higher than a simple cry: "I love You, God."

I do not pray for success. I ask for faithfulness.

And I will betroth you to Me in faithfulness. Then you will know the Lord.
Hosea 2:20 NASB

103

Therefore, my beloved, be steadfast, immovable, always excelling in the work of the Lord....
1 Corinthians 15:58 NRSV

Pray devoutly, but hammer stoutly.

Pray to God, but row for the shore.

Whatever you do, do your work heartily, as for the Lord rather than for men.
Colossians 3:23
NASB

But to us, O Lord, be merciful, for we have waited for you. Be our strength each day and our salvation in the time of trouble.
Isaiah 33:2 TLB

Don't pray for tasks suited to your capacity. Pray for capacity suited to your tasks.

O, do not pray for easy lives. Pray to be stronger men.

Those who hope in the Lord will renew their strength.
Isaiah 40:31 NIV

The end of all things is near. Therefore be clear minded and self-controlled so that you can pray.
1 Peter 4:7 NIV

~

We are living in dangerous times and if there was ever a time when we need to pray, it's now.

More can be done by prayer than anything else, prayer is our greatest weapon.

Wherefore take unto you the whole armour of God...Praying always with all prayer and supplication.
Ephesians 6:13,18

109

Thou art my hope, O Lord God ...[Thou] shalt quicken me again, and shalt bring me up again from the depths of the earth.
Psalm 71:5,20

A good man's prayers will from the deepest dungeon climb heaven's height, and bring a blessing down.

110

I have been driven many times to my knees by the overwhelming conviction that I had nowhere else to go.

The eternal God is your refuge and dwelling place, and underneath are the everlasting arms.
Deuteronomy 33:27 AMP

The labor of the righteous leads to life.
Proverbs 10:16
NKJV

True prayer brings a person's will into accordance with God's will, not the other way around.

We can expect big trouble when we try to answer our own prayers.

O Jehovah, answer my prayers...for I am in deep trouble. Quick! Come and save me.
Psalm 69:16,17
TLB

But Jesus replied, "Let the little children come to me, and don't prevent them. For of such is the Kingdom of Heaven." Matthew 19:14 TLB

Genuine prayer is never "good works," an exercise or pious attitude, but it is always the prayer of a child to a Father.

Prayer is the opening of your heart to God as to a friend. You speak to Him, and He speaks back — if you'll but listen!

Be still and know that I am God!
Psalm 46:10

115

The weapons of our warfare are not carnal but mighty in God for pulling down strongholds.
2 Corinthians 10:4 NKJV

We possess a divine artillery that silences the enemy and inflicts upon him the damage he would inflict upon us.

Prayer is the preface to the book of Christian living; the text of the new life sermon; the girding on of the armor for battle.

Put on the whole armor of God, that you may be able to stand against the wiles of the devil... praying always with all prayer and supplication in the Spirit.
Ephesians 6:11,18
NKJV

God's Little Instruction Book on Prayer

Now to him who is able to do immeasurably more than all we ask or imagine, according to his power that is at work within us....
Ephesians 3:20
NIV

When we depend on man, we get what man can do; when we depend on prayer, we get what God can do.

118

Prayer is a powerful thing because God has bound it to Himself.

And I will do whatever you ask in my name, so that the Son may bring glory to the Father.
John 14:13 NIV

Thou hast enclosed me behind and before, and laid Thy hand upon me.
Psalm 139:5 NASB

Prayer serves as an edge and border to preserve the web of life from unraveling.

Prayer is God's way of doing God's will.

So the man of God interceded with the Lord, and the king's hand was restored and became as it was before.
1 Kings 13:6 NIV

If therefore you are presenting your offering at the altar, and there remember that your brother has something against you, leave your offering there before the altar, and go your way; first be reconciled to your brother, and then come and present your offering.
Matthew 5:23-24
NASB

We cannot separate our prayer from how we treat other people.

We do pray for mercy, and that same prayer doth teach us all to render the deeds of mercy.

Blessed are the merciful: for they shall obtain mercy.
Matthew 5:7

Our Father which art in heaven, Hallowed be thy name.
Matthew 6:9 KJV

The Lord's Prayer... may be committed to memory quickly, but it is slowly learned *by heart.*

If you can't pray as you want to, pray as you can. God knows what you mean.

..."Lord, help me!"
Matthew 15:25
NIV

Keep praying earnestly for all Christians everywhere.
Ephesians 6:18
TLB

The best way to remember people is in prayer.

He prayeth best, who loveth best.

Dear friends, since God so loved us, we also ought to love one another.
1 John 4:11 NIV

For God is my witness, whom I serve with my spirit in the gospel of his Son, that without ceasing I make mention of you always in my prayers.
Romans 1:9

Men may spurn our appeals, reject our message, oppose our arguments, despise our persons, but they are helpless against our prayers.

"Christian! seek not yet repose," Hear thy guardian angel say; Thou art in the midst of foes — "Watch and pray."

Take heed, watch and pray.
Mark 13:33 NKJV

129

I rise before dawn and cry for help; I have put my hope in your word.
Psalm 119:147
NIV

I have so much to do today that I shall spend the first three hours in prayer.

D o not face a day until you have faced God.

O God,...early will I seek thee: my soul thirsteth for thee, my flesh longeth for thee in a dry and thirsty land, where no water is.
Psalm 63:1

My soul waits in silence for God only; from Him is my salvation.
Psalm 62:1 NASB

There are moments when, whatever be the attitude of the body, the soul is on its knees.

If you want to know about God, there is only one way to do it: Get down on your knees.

If any of you lacks wisdom, let him ask of God, who gives to all liberally and without reproach, and it will be given to him.
James 1:5 NKJV

133

Daniel, who is one of the exiles from Judah, pays no attention to you, O king, or to the decree you put in writing. He still prays three times a day.
Daniel 6:13 NIV

If you find it hard to stand for Jesus, try kneeling first.

You will not stumble
while on your knees.

*Uphold my steps
in Your paths,
That my footsteps
may not slip.*
Psalm 17:5 NKJV

135

Giving thanks always for all things unto God and the Father in the name of our Lord Jesus Christ.
Ephesians 5:20

Life's best outlook is a prayerful uplook.

A single grateful thought raised to heaven is the most perfect prayer.

Praise the Lord! Oh, give thanks to the Lord, for He is good! For His mercy endures forever. Psalm 106:1 NKJV

Evening, and morning, and at noon, will I pray, and cry aloud: and he shall hear my voice.
Psalm 55:17

No day is well spent without communication with God.

He who runs from God in the morning will scarcely find Him the rest of the day.

Let me see your kindness to me in the morning, for I am trusting you. Show me where to walk, for my prayer is sincere.
Psalm 143:8 TLB

139

You have put gladness in my heart...I will both lie down in peace, and sleep; For You alone, O Lord, make me dwell in safety.
Psalm 4:7,8 NKJV

In the morning, prayer is the key that opens to us the treasures of God's mercies and blessings; in the evening, it is the key that shuts us up under His protection and safeguard.

Prayer should be the key of the morning and the bolt of the night.

O Lord, the God of my salvation, I have cried to You for help by day; at night I am in Your presence. Psalm 88:1 AMP

My help comes from the Lord, who made heaven and earth.
Psalm 121:2 NRSV

Good endings come from prayerful beginnings.

Famous Prayers

Our Father which art in heaven,
Hallowed be thy name.
Thy kingdom come.
Thy will be done in earth, as it is in heaven.
Give us this day our daily bread.
And forgive us our debts, as we forgive our debtors.
And lead us not into temptation, but deliver us from evil:
For thine is the kingdom, and the power, and the glory, for ever.
Amen.

~

The Lord's Prayer
Matthew 6:9-13

O Lord, heavenly Father, in whom is the fullness of light and wisdom, enlighten our minds by your Holy Spirit, and give us grace to receive your Word with reverence and humility, without which no one can understand your truth.... Amen.

— John Calvin

O Lord, you are never weary of doing me good. Let me never be weary of doing you service. But as you have pleasure in the prosperity of your servants, so let me take pleasure in the service of my Lord, and abound in your work, and in your love and praise evermore. O fill up all that is wanting, reform whatever is amiss in me, perfect the thing that concerns me. Let the witness of your pardoning love ever abide in my heart.

— *John Wesley*

Before I lay me down to sleep, I give myself to Christ to keep.
Four corners to my bed, four Angels overspread:
One at the head, one at the feet, and two to guard me while I sleep.

I go by sea, I go by land, the Lord made me with his right hand.
If any danger come to me, sweet Jesus Christ, deliver me.
He is the branch and I'm the flower, may God send me a
happy hour.

— A Traditional Prayer

L ord, make me an instrument of your peace;
Where there is hatred, let me sow love;
Where there is injury, pardon;
Where there is doubt, faith;
Where there is despair, hope;
Where there is darkness, light;
Where there is sadness, joy.

O Divine Master,
grant that I may not so much seek
to be consoled, as to console;
to be understood, as to understand;
to be loved, as to love;
for it is in giving that we receive,
it is in pardoning that we are pardoned,
it is in dying that we are born to eternal life.

— *St. Francis of Assisi*

May the strength of God pilot us.
May the power of God preserve us.
May the wisdom of God instruct us.
May the hand of God protect us.
May the way of God direct us.
May the shield of God defend us.
May the host of God guard us

     - against the snares of the evil ones.
     - against temptations of the world.

May Christ be with us!
May Christ be before us!
May Christ be in us,
Christ be over all!
May thy salvation, Lord, always be ours,
This day, O Lord, and evermore.

— Attributed to St. Patrick

Dear Jesus,
Help us to spread your fragrance everywhere we go. Flood our souls with your spirit and life. Penetrate and possess our whole being so utterly that our lives may be a radiance of yours . . . Let us thus praise you in the way you love best by shining on those around us. Let us preach you without preaching, not by words, but by example by the catching force, the sympathetic influence of what we do, the evident fullness of the love our hearts bear to you.

— *Mother Teresa*

I kneel before the Father, from whom the whole family in heaven and on earth derives its name. I pray that out of his glorious riches he may strengthen you with power through his Spirit in your inner being, so that Christ may dwell in your hearts through faith. And I pray that you, being rooted and established in love, may have power, together with all the saints, to grasp how wide and long and high and deep is the love of Christ, and to know this love that surpasses knowledge — that you may be filled to the measure of all the fulness of God.

∾

— *Paul's Prayer for the Ephesians (Paraphrased)*
  Ephesians 3:14-19

God bless all those that I love;
God bless all those that love me;
God bless all those that love those that I love
and all those that love those that love me.

∾

— *Sixteenth Century New England Sampler*

References

Acknowledgments

Oswald Chambers (4), Henri Nouwen (5,63), Eliza M. Hickok (7), Lorrie Morgan (8), Benjamin S. Carson, M.D. (9), Alexander Maclaren (15), Abraham Joshua Heschel (17), Francis Fenelon (18), Frederick Buechner (19), Thomas Brooks (20,21,22), Martin Luther (23,111,130), G. Ashton Oldham (24), Joseph Fort Newton (25), Leonard Ravenhill (26), Charles L. Allen (27), Charles Spurgeon (28), George Failing (29), William McGill (31), Alexander Whyte (32), Dan Matthews (33), Ambrose (36), Thomas Fuller (38), Dorothy Thompson (39), Teresa of Avila (40), Hosea Ballou (41), Montaigne (42), William Poole (43), Thomas Hooker (44), H.M.S. Richards (45), Julian of Norwich (47), Richard C. Trench (48), James O. Fraser (49), William G. Johnsson (50), Soren Kierkegaard (51), George E. Rees (52), William Cary (53), John Bunyan (54,61,139), Hannah More (55,82), George Appleton (56), O. Hallesby (57), Andrew Murray (59,69,123), Samuel Osgood (64), W.E. Sangster and Leslie

Davison (68), Merlin R. Carothers (71), Peter Deyneka (72), Jack Hayford (74), Edward P. Roe (75), Madam De Gasparin (76), D. L. Moody (77), John Aikman Wallace (79), Julius Hare (81), Jean Ingelow (83), Joseph Hall (84), Mark Hopkins (85), Rabbi Judah Halevi (87), Morris Venden (89), Alfred, Lord Tennyson (90), Lord Samuel (92), Bernard (93), Wesley L. Duewel (96,115), Clement of Alexandria (97), Henry Ward Beecher (98), John Owen (99), Richard Monckton Milnes (101), Louis Cassels (102), Mother Teresa (103,152), Sir William Gurney Benham (104), Phillips Brooks (107), Billy Graham (108,109), Joanna Baillie (110), Abraham Lincoln (111), Janette Oke (113), Dietrich Bonhoeffer (114), Corrie ten Boom (116), Austin Phelps (117), Robert Hall (120), John F. D. Maurice (124), Vance Havner (125), Samuel Taylor Coleridge (127), Sidlow Baxter (128), Charlotte Elliott (129), Victor Hugo (132), Archbishop Fulton Sheen (133), Gotthold Ephraim Lessing (137), John Calvin (145), John Wesley (146), St. Francis of Assisi (148,149), St. Patrick (150,151).

Additional Copies of this book and other titles in the
God's Little Instruction Book series are available at your local bookstore.

God's Little Instruction Book
God's Little Instruction Book II
God's Little Instruction Book for Mom
God's Little Instruction Book for Dad
God's Little Instruction Book for Graduates
God's Little Instruction Book for Students
God's Little Instruction Book for Kids
God's Little Instruction Book for Couples
God's Little Instruction Book for Women
God's Little Instruction Book for the Workplace
God's Little Instruction Book — Special Gift Edition
God's Little Instruction Book Daily Calendar

HONOR
B O O K S

Tulsa, Oklahoma